Abdul Salam's
Secret Curry Cookbook

Abdul Salam & Simon Rigby

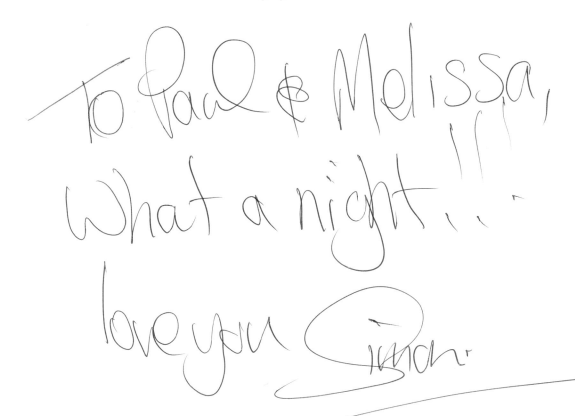

To Paul & Melissa,
What a night...
love you Simon

First Published in July 2005
By Elford House Publishing
East Wing, Elford House
Elford, Staffordshire B79 9BN

Copyrite © Elford House Publishing

Origination by SB Associates, Great Barr, Birmingham B44 8RA
Photography by Alan Williamson
Printed by Howson Print Limited, Aldridge, West Midlands

About Abdul Salam

Abdul Salam was born in Keshobpur Jogannath-pur, Sunamgonj Bangladesh in 1959. As a young boy he worked in his grandfather's restaurant, learning the trade and the secrets of spices. He moved to the U.K. in 1975 where he joined the kitchen staff at an Indian restaurant in Edgware. He later moved to Cheltenham where he opened his first restaurant, The Akash. His reputation as a skilled chef was soon confirmed and the restaurant flourished.

In 1982 he opened restaurants in Tipton and later Stourport on Severn. In 1990 he opened the Eastern Eye restaurant in Lichfield, Staffordshire. This was at the height of the 1990 elections and the Eastern Eye became hugely popular with politicians and the media, the latter of which turned the restaurant into their unofficial election base.

Over the following decade Abdul's reputation continued to grow and the Eastern Eye was regularly frequented by the famous. In 1999 Abdul won the coveted title of "Britain's Number One Curry Chef." Later, the same year, the Eastern Eye won the title of Britain's top Bangladeshi Restaurant.

In 2000 he entered the Guinness Book of Records for creating the world's biggest curry. Now with four restaurants in the Midlands Abdul has decided to reveal some of the secrets of Bangladeshi cuisine in this, his first cookery book. "People are always disappointed", he says, "when the curry they make at home does not taste like the one at their local Indian restaurant. Now, by following my recipes, they will."

Recipe Contents

Sauces and Starters

Abdul's special mint sauce   9
Tandoori king prawn   10
Chicken tikka   13
Onion bhaji   14
Sheek kebab   17

Vegetable Dishes

Gouka aloo potatoes   18
Spicy chickpeas   21
Bhindi bhaji okra   22
Vegetable gajjor   25
Vegetable biryani   26

Meat and Poultry Dishes

Bazari lamb   29
Chicken passanda   32
Keshobpuri lamb   35
Tajan palak   36
Special chicken pathia   39
Chicken tikka masala   40
Chicken kashmir   43
Jungle murgha partridge   44
Chicken dopiaza   47
Chicken korma   48

Fish/Shellfish Dishes

Pani ka raja   51
Ananash supreme   52
Spicy sea bass   55
Cox bazaar king prawn   56

How to use this cookbook

The curry recipes in my book are exactly the same as the ones we prepare in my restaurants. The ingredients are the same and the fast preparation methods are the ones we use. As well as restaurant favourites I have introduced a number of new dishes which I hope you find exciting. Whether you are an experienced cook or trying to make curries for the first time, I believe you will not find an easier to follow recipe book.

The measures used throughout are simple. There are two types - British standard measures giving a tablespoon measure as 15ml, a teaspoon measure as 5ml and a cup at 250ml. The other is the "Abdul standard measure" – a "pinch" which is just that, and a "handful", which is just that, a handful. You will also see that I state when to add the herbs and spices during cooking. This is important and where I believe people go wrong. Spices need to cook for different times, not just be thrown into a pan and burnt to a crisp!

Certain techniques I use will surprise some of you but this is how we do it in a fast kitchen with a menu the size of "War and Peace." I know a lot of curry lovers like hot curries. If you want any of the dishes hotter then add chilli powder during the middle or at the end of the cooking process. I appreciate personal taste.

Herbs and spices used throughout the book are my favourites. Always use fresh ginger and fresh garlic, do not chop garlic and ginger unless it is crushed first as crushing them releases all the flavour. The chopped tomatoes used are those that you buy in a tin but before using them put them in a blender or whisk them to break them down even more – you will notice the difference in the curry's texture. Most of the herbs and spices are available from supermarkets, the ones you will have to get from specialist stores are chaat masala, panchphoran and garam flour.

In total I use 22 different herbs and spices. If you want to stock up so that you can make any dish at any time, here is the list: Fresh ginger, turmeric, cumin seed, cumin powder, coriander seed, fresh coriander, garam flour, garam masala, garlic, cloves, fresh mint, oregano, panchphoran, chaat masala, fenugreek, chilli powder, almond powder, bay leaves, dill, pepper corns, cardamom pods and tandoori paste.

Finally, invest in a rice cooker; they are the simplest, foolproof way of cooking perfect rice every time. Don't ruin a dish just because of the rice.

Enjoy,
Abdul Salam

Abduls Special Mint Sauce

INGREDIENTS

900g fresh plain yoghurt

Handful fresh, chopped mint

$^1/_2$ cup mango chutney

Handful fresh, chopped coriander

$^1/_2$ cooking apple, peeled, cored and chopped

1 tsp salt

6 tbsp honey

2 tbsp olive oil

2 fresh, red chillies

METHOD

Place all the ingredients in a blender and blend until creamy, (approximately 10 seconds). This is the most simple of sauces, variations of which are found in all Indian restaurants. It can be used as an accompaniment to any of the starters listed in this cook book or as a dip for papadums and naan bread.

Tandoori King Prawn

METHOD

Butterfly the king prawns and set aside. To make the marinade, mix all the ingredients together in a bowl and lastly add the king prawns, making sure they are well coated. Leave to marinate in the fridge for 1 hour. Grill on a medium heat for 5 minutes either side. Serve with a crisp salad. This marinade can be used for any grilled or barbequed fish.

INGREDIENTS

8 large king prawns, cut open (2 per person)

2 cm ginger, peeled and crushed

4 cloves garlic, peeled and crushed

1 tsp salt

Juice $1/2$ lemon

1 tsp cumin

1 tsp coriander

1 tbsp fresh, chopped coriander

2 tbsp vegetable oil

1 tsp turmeric

4 tbsp plain yoghurt

Chicken Tikka

SERVES 4

INGREDIENTS

4 chicken breasts cut into 1 cm cubes

MARINADE

1 ¹/₂ cm ginger, peeled and crushed

5 cloves garlic, peeled and crushed

2 tbsp olive oil

1 tsp cumin

1 tsp coriander

3 tbsp fresh, chopped coriander

4 tbsp plain yoghurt

1 tsp salt

1 tbsp fresh mint, chopped

¹/₂ tsp oregano

METHOD

Mix all the ingredients together and add the chicken pieces to the marinade. Leave for a minimum of 2 hours in the fridge or preferably over night. Grill the chicken on a medium heat for 10 – 15 minutes until cooked, but not dry. Pour over any of the remaining marinade during grilling. Serve with a crisp salad.

Onion Bhaji

METHOD

Boil the lentils in water until cooked. Set aside. In a bowl mix together the onion, ginger, turmeric, salt, cumin, coriander and the chopped green chillies. Add the lentils and mix well. Beat in the egg until well mixed. Add the garam flour and mix all the ingredients together. Roll the mixture into balls and deep fry until golden brown. Serve with the lemon wedges and cucumber slices.

INGREDIENTS

2 large onions, peeled and finely chopped

2 cm ginger, peeled, crushed and finely chopped

$1/2$ cup red lentils

2 tsp turmeric

$1/2$ tsp salt

1 tsp cumin

1 tsp coriander

2 green chillies, finely chopped

1 egg

1 cup garam flour

Lemon wedge and cucumber slices to garnish

Sheek Kebab

MAKES 8 PIECES

INGREDIENTS

450g of minced lamb
alternatively minced beef, chicken or pork)

2 cm ginger, peeled and finely chopped

4 cloves garlic, peeled and crushed

1/2 large, finely chopped onion

1 tbsp whole coriander seeds, crushed

1 tsp cumin powder

1 tsp coriander

1 tsp salt

1 tsp turmeric

2 tbsp fresh, chopped coriander

Lemon quarters for serving

8 wooden skewers

METHOD

In a bowl add all the spices to the meat and mix well. Wet the skewers to prevent them from burning when grilling. Take a portion of the meat mixture and roll it around the skewer and shape it until it forms a log. Leave approximately 3 cm of the skewer exposed so the kebab can be turned easily under the grill. Repeat the process with the remaining mixture. Grill the kebabs on a medium heat turning regularly for 10 minutes. Alternatively, roll the log shapes without the skewers and cook on a lightly oiled cast iron skillet. Serve with lemon quarters.

Gouka Aloo Potatoes

SERVES 4

METHOD

Parboil the potatoes and set aside. With the heat on high, put the oil in a large frying pan and add the chopped garlic, ginger, dried chillies and peeled chopped tomatoes. After 20 seconds turn the heat down to low and add the fenugreek, oregano, salt, sugar, turmeric, coriander, panchphoran, cumin, garam masala and dill. Stir the ingredients together with the heat turned to high to get the spices to mix. Work into a paste, stirring all the time.

After 30 seconds, turn the heat down and add the water. Turn the heat back up and stir. After 15 seconds add the yoghurt, coconut flour and chaat masala. After 1 minute turn the heat down to a simmer and add the potatoes and fresh coriander and stir gently for a further minute before serving.

INGREDIENTS

2 large potatoes, quartered

4 tbsp vegetable oil

2 cloves garlic, peeled and crushed

2 cm fresh ginger, peeled, crushed and finely chopped

4 dried chillies

4 tbsp chopped, peeled tomatoes, blended

$1/2$ tsp fenugreek

Pinch of oregano

$1/2$ tsp salt

Pinch of sugar

$1/2$ tsp turmeric

1 tsp coriander

1 tsp panchphoran

1 tsp cumin

$1/2$ tsp garam masala

Pinch of dill

3 tbsp water

4 tbsp plain yoghurt

2 tbsp coconut flour or ground coconut

Pinch of chaat masala

Pinch of fresh, chopped coriander

Spicy Chickpeas

SERVES 4

INGREDIENTS

1 425g tin chickpeas, drained

$^1/_2$ tsp salt

1 $^1/_2$ tbsp vegetable oil

1 egg

2 cm ginger, peeled, crushed and chopped

1 small onion finely chopped

1 $^1/_2$ tbsp chopped, peeled tomatoes, blended

1 tsp turmeric

1 tsp chilli powder (optional)

$^1/_2$ tsp cumin

$^1/_2$ tsp coriander

3 tbsp plain yoghurt

METHOD

Hard boil the egg and set aside. Heat the oil in a pan and add the onion and ginger. Stir on a medium heat for 30 seconds before adding the chopped tomatoes. Stir for a further 10 seconds and add the turmeric, cumin, and coriander. Continue to stir while bringing to the boil. At this stage you may add the chilli powder if you prefer a hotter version of this dish. Bring to the boil and add the chickpeas. Crush the egg into pieces and add to the pan together with the yoghurt. Slowly bring back to the boil and serve.

Bhindi Bhaji Okra

SERVES 4

METHOD

Heat the oil in the pan and add the chopped onion and bay leaf and sir until the onion is golden brown. Add the chopped tomatoes, cumin, coriander, turmeric, panchphoran and stir. Bring to the boil and toss in the okra. Stir for 30 seconds and reduce the heat to a simmer and leave for 1 $\frac{1}{2}$ minutes. Serve at once.

INGREDIENTS

500g Okra (lady's fingers) washed and cut into strips

2 tbsp vegetable oil

1 bay leaf

1 large, finely chopped onion

$\frac{1}{2}$ tsp cumin

$\frac{1}{2}$ tsp coriander

1 tsp turmeric

$\frac{1}{2}$ tsp panchphoran

2 tbsp chopped, peeled tomatoes, blended

Vegetable Gajjor

SERVES 4

INGREDIENTS

2 ¹/₂ tbsp vegetable oil

1 courgette, sliced into 2 cm chunks

¹/₂ tsp salt

2 tbsp chopped, peeled tomatoes, blended

1 medium carrot, coarsely chopped

1 small spring cabbage, coarsely chopped

1 aubergine, sliced into 2 cm chunks

1 bay leaf

¹/₂ tsp panchphoran

1 ¹/₂ tsp turmeric

¹/₂ tsp cumin

1 tsp coriander

4 tbsp plain yoghurt

¹/₂ tsp honey

¹/₂ tsp sugar

¹/₂ tsp almond powder

2 tbsp coconut milk

2 tbsp fresh, chopped coriander

1 tomato, quartered

METHOD

In a large pan boil the courgette, carrot and cabbage until just cooked but still crunchy. Set aside. Deep fry the aubergine until cooked (approximately 1 minute) and set aside.

Heat the oil in a pan and add the salt, bay leaf and chopped tomatoes. Stirring all the time, add the panchphoran, turmeric, cumin and coriander. Stir for one minute on a medium heat and add the yoghurt, almond powder, fresh tomatoes and coconut milk. Add the cooked vegetables and 1 cup of the vegetable water, honey and sugar. Stir and bring to the boil. Serve garnished with the fresh coriander.

Vegetable Biryani

METHOD

Cook the rice in a rice cooker adding the correct amounts for 4 people. This is the best way to cook rice and ensures perfect results every time for this dish. Once cooked, keep warm.

In water, boil the swede and potatoes together until cooked but firm. Boil the courgette and sweet potato together until cooked but firm. Boil the peas on their own, until cooked. Drain the vegetables and set aside.

Heat the oil in a large, non-stick saucepan. Stirring all the time, add the bay leaf, cumin, coriander, panchphoran, turmeric, fresh coriander, cashew nuts, salt, honey and lemon juice. With the heat on medium add the vegetables and mix together quickly. Turn the heat to high and add the rice. Mix together and serve.

INGREDIENTS

1 courgette, coarsely chopped

1 swede, peeled and coarsely chopped

1 large potato, peeled and coarsely chopped

1 large sweet potato, peeled and coarsely chopped

$1/2$ cup garden peas

Basmati rice (for 4 people)

4 tbsp vegetable oil

1 bay leaf

$1/2$ tsp cumin

1 tsp coriander

$1/2$ tsp panchphoran

1 tsp turmeric

Handful fresh, chopped coriander

1 handful cashew nuts

1 tsp salt

$1/2$ tsp honey

Juice $1/2$ lemon

Bazari Lamb

SERVES 4

INGREDIENTS

450g lamb cut into 2 cm cubes
4 tbsp vegetable oil
1 onion coarsely chopped
1 green pepper, coarsely chopped
6 tbsp of peeled, chopped tomatoes, blended
$1/2$ tsp salt
1 tsp sugar
2 tsp turmeric
3 cups water
1 tsp fenugreek
$1/2$ tsp oregano
1 $1/2$ tsp coriander
1 tsp panchphoran
2 tsp cumin
1 $1/2$ tsp garam masala
Pinch of dill
2 red, dried chillies
5 tbsp plain yoghurt
1 tbsp fresh, chopped coriander
1 tbsp finely ground almonds
1 tbsp coconut flour or ground coconut
Juice of $1/2$ lemon
1 tomato, quartered.

METHOD

Add the oil to a large frying pan and when hot add the lamb, onion, pepper and chopped tomatoes and stir. Add the salt, sugar and turmeric and stir until they are all combined. After 10 seconds add two cups of water, stir and leave on a medium heat for 45 minutes. Add more water if the dish begins to dry out.

Stir in the fenugreek, oregano, panchphoran, coriander, cumin, garam masala, red dried chillies and dill. Gently add half the remaining cup of water to the side of the pan, stir and bring to the boil. Add half the fresh chopped coriander, yoghurt, ground almonds and coconut flour, stir and reduce the heat and allow to simmer for 35 minutes. Add the tomato quarters and lemon juice and leave for a further 5 minutes. Garnish with the remaining coriander before serving.

EASTERN EYE

Monster samosa hots up charity

By Martin Banks

NEC SHOW IS HOT DATE FOR CURRY CHEF

By Jim Entwistle

a stir

King Abdul and his spicy wish

By ROB DAVIES

A

mercury

Award for champion curry

Abdul cooks up a top award

Half-term family money-savers

Currying with a

Changes to raise rates of recycling

Mercury News

City curry king meets an admiring princess

By Andy Kerr

Toy joy

Abdul plans a monster massala

Mercury News

EASTERN EYE

Chicken Passanda

METHOD

In a heavy pan mix together all the ingredients except for the chopped banana, mango juice, sultanas and fresh chopped coriander. When mixed add the chicken and mix until coated. Place the pan on a medium heat and stir in the mango juice. Bring to the boil, stirring occasionally. When boiled add the banana, sultanas and fresh chopped coriander and reduce the heat to low. Heat through, stirring all the time.

INGREDIENTS

4 chicken breasts cut into 2 cm chunks

8 tbsp olive oil

2 cm ginger, peeled and finely crushed

4 cloves garlic, peeled and crushed

1 1/2 tsp salt

3 tbsp sugar

8 tbsp chopped, peeled tomatoes, blended

1 1/2 tbsp turmeric

1/2 tbsp cumin

1 tbsp coriander

1/2 tbsp garam masala

1 1/2 cups plain yoghurt

1 1/2 cups coconut milk

5 tbsp almond powder

1/2 cup water

2 bananas, peeled and coarsely chopped

2 tbsp fresh chopped coriander

1 cup thick mango juice (fresh or tinned)

Handful of sultanas

Keshobpuri Lamb

SERVES 6-8

INGREDIENTS

1 whole leg of lamb

$1/2$ cup olive oil

1 tbsp cumin

2 tbsp coriander

3 cm ginger, peeled and crushed

1 whole garlic, peeled and crushed

1 $1/2$ tsp salt

$1/2$ tbsp garam masala

1 tsp oregano

6 tbsp plain yoghurt

1 handful fresh, chopped coriander

Juice of $1/2$ lemon

METHOD

Score the leg of lamb all over and set aside. In the order listed, mix all the ingredients together in a bowl. Line a baking tray with 2 -3 layers of cooking foil to stop the under-side of the leg from burning during cooking. Smother the lamb with the mixture working it into the scored flesh. Wrap the lamb tightly in cooking foil sealing the edges. Place the lamb on the baking tray and place in a pre-heated oven at 220°c/425°F/Gas Mark 7. After 2 hours reduce the heat to 180°c (for fan assisted ovens adjust temperature/cooking times accordingly).

Tajan Palak

SERVES 4

METHOD

In a heavy saucepan, boil the beef in water for one hour. The heat should be between low and medium throughout cooking. After the hour remove the meat with a slotted spoon and set aside.

In a large saucepan mix together the onions, ginger, garlic, vegetable oil, bay leaves, pepper corns, cloves, cardamom pods, star anise, cumin, coriander, turmeric, lemon juice, tamarind juice, sugar, salt, spinach and chopped tomatoes. When well mixed cook over a medium heat for 10 minutes, stirring occasionally. If the mixture begins to dry out add water, a little at a time. After a further 5 minutes add the meat and yoghurt and mix well. After a further 10 minutes stir in the fresh coriander and increase the heat to high for 1 minute, stirring all the time. Reduce the heat to a mild simmer for 5 minutes before serving.

INGREDIENTS

450g lean, top side beef, cubed.

3 cm peeled, chopped fresh ginger

6 cloves garlic, peeled and crushed

1 onion, coarsely chopped

8 tbsp vegetable oil

2 bay leaves

8 black pepper corns

10 cloves

6 green cardamom pods

1 large star anise

1 1/2 tsp cumin

2 tsp coriander

1 tbsp turmeric

Juice 1/2 lemon

1 tbsp tamarind juice

1 tbsp sugar

1 tsp salt

2 cups chopped, peeled tomatoes, blended

6 tbsp plain yoghurt

2 large bunches spinach

Handful fresh, chopped coriander

Special Chicken Pathia

SERVES 4

INGREDIENTS

2 chicken breasts cut into 5 cm cubes
4 tbsp vegetable oil
4 small dried red chillies
2 cloves garlic, peeled and crushed
1/2 green pepper coarsely chopped
1 small onion coarsely chopped
2 cm ginger, peeled and crushed
1 tsp fenugreek
1/2 tsp oregano
4 tbsp peeled, chopped tomatoes, blended
1/2 tsp salt
1 tsp sugar
1 tsp ground coriander
1/2 tsp panchphoran
1 tsp cumin
1/2 tsp garam masala
Pinch of dill
1 tsp turmeric
4 small fresh green chillies finely chopped
5 tbsp plain yoghurt
1 tbsp finely ground almonds
1 tbsp coconut flour or ground coconut
4 tbsp water
Pinch fresh chopped coriander
Juice of 1/2 lemon
1 tomato quartered

METHOD

Heat the oil in a large frying pan. When sizzling hot add the 4 small dried chillies and fry for a minute, stirring all the time. Add the garlic, chopped green pepper, chopped onion and ginger. After 10 seconds add the fenugreek, oregano, and chopped tomatoes and continue to stir. Reduce the heat to medium.

After 20 seconds add the chicken breasts, the salt and sugar. Continue to stir for 2 minutes then add the ground coriander, panchphoran, cumin, garam masala, dill and turmeric. Turn the heat up to high, stirring all the time and add the finely chopped chillies, yoghurt, finely ground almonds, coconut flour and water. Turn the heat down to low and add the fresh, chopped coriander, lemon juice and tomato quarters. Stir occasionally while simmering for a further five minutes. Add additional water if the curry begins to dry.

Chicken Tikka Masala

SERVES 4

METHOD

Make the chicken tikka as described in the recipe on page 13 and set aside.

MASALA SAUCE

In a heavy pan mix all the ingredients together, except the almond powder, salt, coconut powder and a pinch of the fresh coriander. Place on a medium heat, stirring all the time, bring to the boil and immediately reduce the heat to a simmer. Stir in the almond powder, salt and coconut powder and bring to the boil. As soon as the sauce begins to boil add the chicken tikka pieces and reduce to a medium heat. The sauce can be diluted to your preferred consistency at this stage by adding water. A sweeter taste can be achieved by adding more sugar or honey. Once the chicken is cooked through serve with the fresh cream and the remaining fresh coriander sprinkled on top.

INGREDIENTS

4 Chicken tikka breasts cut into 2 cm cubes

MASALA SAUCE

6 tbsp vegetable oil

1 $^{1}/_{2}$ cups chopped, peeled tomatoes, blended

4 cups plain yoghurt

$^{1}/_{2}$ cooking apple, peeled, cored and finely crushed

$^{1}/_{2}$ tbsp cumin

1 tsp sugar

$^{1}/_{2}$ tbsp coriander

$^{1}/_{2}$ tbsp turmeric

2 tbsp double cream

4-5 tbsp fresh, chopped coriander

4 tbsp tandoori paste

3 tbsp almond powder

1 tsp salt

3 tbsp coconut powder or ground coconut

Chicken Kashmir

SERVES 4

INGREDIENTS

4 chicken breasts cut into 2 cm chunks

8 tbsp olive oil

2 cm ginger, peeled and finely crushed

4 cloves garlic, peeled and crushed

1 $\frac{1}{2}$ tsp salt

1 tbsp sugar

8 tbsp peeled, chopped tomatoes, blended

1 $\frac{1}{2}$ tbsp turmeric

$\frac{1}{2}$ tbsp cumin

1 tbsp coriander

$\frac{1}{2}$ tbsp garam masala

1 $\frac{1}{2}$ cups plain yoghurt

$\frac{1}{2}$ cup coconut milk

3 tbsp almond powder

$\frac{1}{2}$ cup water

2 bananas, peeled and coarsely chopped

2 tbsp fresh chopped coriander

METHOD

In a heavy pan mix together all the ingredients except for the chicken, chopped banana and fresh, chopped coriander. When mixed add the chicken and mix until coated. Place the pan on a medium heat, stirring occasionally. When boiled add the banana and fresh chopped coriander and reduce the heat to low. Stir for 30 seconds before serving.

Jungle Murgha Partridge

SERVES 2

METHOD

Roast the partridge in a medium oven for approximately 1 hour. Check the bird is cooked using a meat thermometer or meat skewer. The bird will be cooked when clear juices run out. If necessary, cook for a further half an hour. Set aside and cover to keep warm.

In a saucepan mix all the ingredients together in the order listed with the exception of the honey and water. Place on a medium heat and stir until the mixture begins to boil then add the honey and water and mix well. Once boiled, remove from the heat and pour over the bird and carve.

INGREDIENTS

1 small partridge, dressed

4 tbsp olive oil

2 cm fresh ginger, peeled and crushed

4 cloves garlic, peeled and crushed

5 tbsp peeled chopped tomatoes, blended

3 tbsp fresh, plain yoghurt

Juice $1/2$ lemon

$1/2$ tsp cumin

$1/2$ tsp garam masala

$1/2$ tsp coriander

1 tsp turmeric

$1/2$ tsp salt

2 small onions, chopped

1 tsp honey

4 tbsp water

Chicken Dopiaza

SERVES 4

INGREDIENTS

4 chicken breasts cut into 2 cm cubes

$^1/_2$ cup olive oil

2 medium onions, coarsely chopped

$^1/_2$ cup peeled, chopped tomatoes, blended

1 $^1/_2$ tsp cumin

1 $^1/_2$ tsp coriander

2 $^1/_2$ tsp turmeric

1 tsp garam masala

1 tsp salt

2 cups plain yoghurt

1 cup water

4 tbsp almond powder

2 tbsp tamarind juice

Juice $^1/_2$ lemon

METHOD

In a large pan mix all the ingredients (except the chicken) together in the order listed. Cook over a medium heat. As the mixture begins to boil, stir in the chicken and continue to heat so the chicken cooks. Stir occasionally until the mixture becomes semi-dry. At this consistency, remove from the heat and serve.

Chicken Korma

SERVES 4

METHOD

Heat the oil in a heavy pan and add the chopped onion, garlic and ginger. Cook until the onion is golden brown. Reduce the heat to low and add the cashew nuts, sultanas and the 2 tbsp of water. Stir in the chicken and increase the heat to medium, stirring all the time. Add the yoghurt and coconut milk and continue to stir for 10 seconds before adding the almond powder. Mix all the ingredients together well and bring to the boil before adding the cumin, coriander, turmeric, honey and salt. Bring back to the boil before adding the fresh coriander. Stir for 15 seconds before serving.

INGREDIENTS

4 chicken breasts cut into 2 cm chunks

$^1/_2$ cup vegetable oil

1 large onion, chopped

Handful cashew nuts

Handful sultanas (optional)

2 tbsp water

$^1/_2$ garlic bulb, peeled and crushed

4 cm ginger, peeled and crushed

2 cups plain yoghurt

2 cups coconut milk

$^1/_2$ cup honey

1 tsp turmeric

$^1/_2$ cup almond powder

1 tsp cumin

1 $^1/_2$ tsp coriander

1 tsp salt

Handful fresh coriander

Pani Ka Raja

SERVES 4

INGREDIENTS

4 shark steaks about 175g each
1 cup water
Pinch chopped ginger
1 clove garlic, peeled and crushed
4 tbsp vegetable oil
4 tbsp chopped, peeled tomatoes, blended
2 tbsp tamarind juice
Pinch oregano
Pinch fenugreek
1 tsp coriander
$\frac{1}{2}$ tsp cumin
Pinch garam masala
1 tsp turmeric
$\frac{1}{2}$ tsp salt
Pinch sugar
4 tbsp plain yoghurt
Juice of $\frac{1}{2}$ lemon
$\frac{1}{2}$ tbsp coconut flour or ground coconut
$\frac{1}{2}$ tbsp finely ground almonds
1 tomato, quartered
Pinch fresh, chopped coriander
1 coarsely chopped spring onion

METHOD

In a large, heavy pan, add one cup of water and bring to the boil. Add the shark steaks, a pinch of chopped ginger, the garlic and the oil. Continue to boil for a further 2 minutes. Add the chopped tomatoes and tamarind juice and boil for a further 2 minutes. Stir in the oregano, fenugreek, coriander, cumin, garam masala turmeric, salt and sugar and reduce the heat to medium. Add the yoghurt, lemon juice, coconut flour, ground almonds, stir and bring back to the boil. Add the quartered, fresh tomatoes, fresh coriander and chopped spring onion. Still on a medium heat, cook for a further 5 minutes, stirring occasionally.

Ananash Supreme

SERVES 2

METHOD

Slice off the top leaves of the pineapple. Laying the pineapple on its side slice the top off, this will later be used as a lid. Hollow out the inside being careful not to pierce the outside of the pineapple. Set aside.

In a bowl mix together all of the ingredients. Gently fold in the tiger prawns. Spoon the mixture into the pineapple and put the pineapple lid back on.

In a bowl mix the 4 cups of self raising flour with the water. Knead into dough and roll out on a floured surface to make a large naan bread. This will be used to protect the pineapple during cooking and add flavour. It is not to be eaten. Place the pineapple in the centre of the naan and wrap the naan around it until fully covered and sealed. Wrap the naan in foil and seal again.

Place the foil wrapped pineapple on a baking tray and heat in a hot oven (200°c/400°F/Gas Mark 6) for $\frac{1}{2}$ an hour. Remove from the oven and unwrap the foil and naan. Serve as a dish to be enjoyed by two people sharing.

INGREDIENTS

1 pineapple

8 large tiger prawns, washed, shells removed

4 tbsp olive oil

2 cm ginger, peeled and crushed

1 tsp turmeric

$\frac{1}{2}$ tsp cumin

$\frac{1}{2}$ tsp coriander

$\frac{1}{2}$ tsp ground nutmeg

1 handful fresh, chopped coriander

5 tbsp plain, fresh yoghurt

4 tbsp chopped, peeled tomatoes, blended

2 spring onions chopped into 4 cm lengths

Juice of $\frac{1}{2}$ lemon

$\frac{1}{2}$ tsp salt

1 tsp sugar

5 tbsp coconut milk

1 $\frac{1}{2}$ tbsp almond powder

10-12 cashew nuts

Bread mix: 4 cups self raising flour, 1 cup water to make dough

Spicy Sea Bass

SERVES 4

INGREDIENTS

1 whole sea bass

4 whole red chillies

1 tbsp vegetable oil

2 cm ginger, peeled and finely chopped

3 cloves garlic, peeled and crushed

2 spring onions, chopped

1 tbsp fresh coriander, chopped

METHOD

In a fish steamer, cook the sea bass. Refer to the manufacturers instructions for timings. Alternatively the sea bass can be boiled in a large pan of water for 10 minutes. When cooked, wrap in foil and set aside. Heat the oil in a large pan and add the ginger and garlic. Cook until semi golden brown but do not allow to burn. Place the fish on a serving plate and pour over the chilli, garlic and ginger mixture. Garnish with the spring onion and fresh coriander.

Cox Bazaar King Prawn

SERVES 4

METHOD

In a bowl, mix all the ingredients together. Add the king prawns and mix well. Leave to marinate in the fridge for one hour. Place the mixture in a heavy, non stick, pan and cook over a medium heat for approximately 8 minutes, stirring occasionally. Bring to the boil, remove from the heat and serve.

INGREDIENTS

24 large king prawns, shells on

$1/2$ cup olive oil

1 cm ginger, peeled and crushed

4 cloves garlic, peeled and crushed

1 tbsp coriander

$1/2$ tsp cumin

1 cup fish stock

5 tbsp fresh, plain yoghurt

3 tbsp almond powder

1 cup coconut milk

1 tbsp turmeric

Juice of $1/2$ lemon

1 tsp salt

2 cups peeled, chopped tomatoes, blended

1 tbsp sugar

Handful fresh, chopped, coriander

Abdul's Restaurants

Eastern Eye
9, Bird Street, Lichfield, Staffordshire
Tel 01543 254399

Radooni
14, Bailey Street, Stafford, Staffordshire
Tel: 01785 600800

Bukhara (Eastern Fusion)
70 Church Street, Tamworth, Staffordshire
Tel: 01827 64666

Spice 45
Birmingham Road, Meriden
Tel: 01676 522000